It's Your Job

Lisa Raymond

Author's Note:
This book is only a guide to preparing ones-self for possible employment opportunities. It is a compilation of over twenty years of expertise in Human Resources, hiring and educating and is only to assist and guide you in your journey. Therefore, it does not guarantee employment. You are ultimately responsible for resume content, reliability and accountability.

For contact information, please visit:
www.Ethics2Talk.com

Library of Congress 05/2012
Copyright © 2012; 2016 (RLS)

ISBN-13: 9781533483652
ISBN-10: 1533483655

"Thank you" to Gregory Bigelow and Angela Carrier for editing services. Marcus Kirkland for the Ethics2Talk, LLC logo. Photo credit Ahmad Sandidge Photography.

Table of Contents

Sometimes looking for a job can actually be a full-time job. Are you prepared?

Hard Preparation

There is never a time that's a *bad* time to re-evaluate where you are in your life plan. How often do you review your life, where it's going, and more so, how to get there? Are you meeting your smaller goals as you work towards the big picture of your life? When is the last time you looked at the chapters of your life and made changes to your YOU Book?

Talk is simple and cheap, and the reality of life can be cutthroat. Are you ready to face the facts of your life and where it's headed? If you're unhappy with your current situation, it may be time to saddle up and make changes so that you move forward, and not continue to stand in the same place or worse move at a snail's pace. It's time to look beyond the immediate wants you may have and work for the basic needs to secure the future of you and your family.

Many organizations can help in your quest for a better future; they are all within your reach if you step towards them and put time and effort into bettering your skills and hone in on what expertise you have. Sometimes all you have to do is ask for help or ask for the opportunity. Every industry is looking to hire that perfect employee; why shouldn't they hire you?

Your Brand – *Do you have one?*

At some point, we've all heard, "You have to make a good first impression." But did you ever think that the first impression you make could be the last impression that someone will want to see from you? Sometimes there are no second chances to recreate a good first impression.

While a first impression is usually the visual presentation (how you look), how you speak and deal with the interviewer over the phone or in person can be just as important.

In the job market, you are a product in competition with others locally, nationally and globally. What sets you apart from them and their skills? If this is a hard question to answer, you need to create a brand for yourself. A brand is a promise that you make stating what you can do and more so what can be expected from you if offered the job. Your brand should also have the ability to motivate people to ask you more questions as well as continue the conversation. This self-branding is known as an elevator speech.

Think of all of the commercials that you have seen on TV. What stands out? What makes you pick one brand over another? Now, put yourself in the same position like the products that you've seen on TV. Why should someone pick you over another applicant? Your reasoning should be compelling, factual and reliable; while not overwhelming or worse, unbelievable.

When an interviewer starts the conversation, generally they say, "Tell me a little about yourself." This is the time for your elevator speech. It is your time to shine and open the doors of opportunity or have them closed on you.

As an interviewer, 75% of people give the same answer. "I'm hardworking, honest, reliable and dependable." Let's be real, if you had all of those qualities, most likely, you'd be employed, and the company would pay you *not* to leave. So the task becomes how to create interest by briefly giving an honest account of who you are and skills you can share with an organization. Your goal is to sell yourself by finding words that will set you apart from other applicants.

For the interviewer, seeing a more realistic view of what they are purchasing, which is you, will give them a better sense of your skills and how you can support their company if you are hired. With an impressive opening and good first impression, you help the interviewer buy into who you are and ask questions that allow you to showcase your skills better.

When creating your brand, or even re-branding, be innovative and different from the norm. But remember, selling yourself is harder than selling something that you would buy in a store.

Assess your skills and talents so that you know what you have to offer. Discover what makes you interesting enough to get and then hold someone's attention. The following questions can get you on the right track:

1. What exceptional quality do you have that will make someone want to hear what you've got to say?
2. What makes you different than the person who was interviewed before you, or the ones that come after you?
3. What makes you a stand out in your field of expertise?
4. What skills do you bring to the table?

Putting together a prepared and rehearsed elevator speech can take you above the ordinary to become extraordinary and memorable during your interview. As you are talking, be enthusiastic and upbeat. Remember, this is the sales pitch that can possibly get your foot in the door.

Your Cover Letter and Resume

A cover letter is a professional letter used to introduce yourself and to express interest in possible employment with a company. This letter states your purpose while sharing a few of your qualifications, skills, and key accomplishments. The one-page letter should be energetic in nature to help the interviewer see you in a supporting role within their company. A cover letter is an additional part of your branding and should be included when sending your resume.

A resume summarizes your skills and abilities to do a particular job. It is used to highlight past jobs and to summarize your accomplishments in each position you held. In short, a resume, like the cover letter becomes a part of your personal brand.

A lot of times people try to cram everything onto a resume in an attempt to give a complete history of employment. If you do that, what is the point of a potential employer calling you in for an interview? Like a good book, a good resume gives a summary but leaves the reader wanting more. Save some of your best points and accomplishments for the interview.

<u>Popular types of resumes:</u>
- ➤ Paper Resume
- ➤ Curriculum Vitae (CV) more comprehensive than a regular resume (used for academics and research)
- ➤ Online (Email, Monster.com, Indeed.com, etc.)
- ➤ Video or Website Resume

As technology changes, the way resumes are created and shared change as well. It would be in your best interest to keep up with technology, and continuously update your resume with new training, work history and learned skills.

While it is understood what a resume does, remember that how you present your resume can have an effect on whether an employer looks at it or not. Your document should be printed on clean paper. It should be typed, neat, and free of spelling/grammatical errors. Double check your formatting to make sure your spacing is correct and all typesetting matches.

How long should it be? At this time, most organizations like to see a one to two paged resume. However, that may vary depending on the industry you are looking to work in, the skill set and information that may be needed to work in that position, as well as the type of resume that you are using.

Your resume should be to the point, omitting wordiness and catch/buzz phrases. It should detail what you can do, pointing out your strengths and accomplishments, while enticing the person reading it to call you for an interview.

Your cover letter, resume, and reference page should be neat and printed on high-quality paper (even if you previously emailed them).

Resume Content

Heading

Resumes should always have your current contact information located at the top of the page. This includes your name, address, a phone number and an email address. Make sure that your phone number and email are updated and are where you can be reached if called now.

As most people use email, remember to create and utilize an address that is professional and suitable for an employer to view you as a serious candidate. It is recommended to use your first and last name or something that identifies you. Never use an email that may be offensive or negative in nature.

Objective

Years ago, it was a good idea to have an "Objective" but if you've been in the same industry and are looking for a job in that same industry, there is no benefit (other than wasting space) of putting a general objective to your resume unless you are completely changing careers.

Summary of Qualifications

Most resumes don't get fully read, therefore, make it easier on your interviewer to quickly see what you bring to the table regarding skills and experience.

This area is perfect for gathering all of the information that is/was the same in past jobs and putting it in one spot along with valuable skills that you have and accomplishments you have made.

Professional Experience

Here is where you list your work experience. Your most recent job should always go first, followed by former employment in chronological order. Remember to stay away from negative words or phrases that take away from the positives that you bring to an organization. Choose your words carefully staying focused and positive.

Education and Training

Following the employment format, your most recent education should be placed first followed by other education or training you may have received.

High School information isn't necessary unless you've just graduated and are entering the work field.

If you are just graduating from high school or college, place your education before employment history. If you have more recent work experience, your education would be placed after employment history.

Additional Activities

As an added touch, if you have done volunteer work, it can be placed here to show community service.

References Available Upon Request

This should **not** be on the resume. It is (and should be) understood that by coming into an interview, you will have references available if requested.

Remember: There are many styles and formats that you can use for your resume. The following is an example of one type of resume. Regardless of the format that you choose, make sure that you double check your work before sending it out.

JANE DOE   JANE.DOE@YAHOO.COM

1234 State Street · Pittsburgh, PA 15222 · (412) 555-1212

SUMMARY OF QUALIFICATIONS
- List computer skills you may have
- Qualities that you have done in multiple jobs
- Leadership roles you may have taken on

EMPLOYMENT HISTORY

Muto's Auto, Pittsburgh, PA   June 2008 - June 2009
Manager
- Bullet-point your skills so that you draw attention to what services you were able to provide for the company.
- There should only be a couple so that you draw interest.

Joe's Restaurant, Newton, WVA   July 2004 - June 2009
Hostess
- List any relevant skills you had at this position.
- There should only be a couple so that you draw interest.

EDUCATION

Duquesne University, Pittsburgh, PA   2007
Bachelor's in Business Administration

Ever-train, Inc., Pittsburgh, PA   2005
Microsoft Certification

St. John's High School, Newton, WVA   Graduated 2004
(Only list high school if you are a recent graduate with little work experience)

ACTIVITIES

Red Cross, Pittsburgh, PA   Volunteer
Big Brothers Big Sisters, Pittsburgh, PA   Volunteer

Soft Preparation

Now that you've worked on your resume, it's time to look at the actual product which is you.

"What are *soft skills*?" Soft skills are characteristics that a person brings to the table not only in the interview but the job as well. They can be daily interactions with co-workers, common sense decisions, dress, communication skills, and responsibility level just to name a few. While many people have the "hard skills" necessary for a job, they can easily be lacking in soft skills.

Take a long hard look in the mirror. See the physical package that you present to other people. Could it be time to make a full-hearted change so that others see the best that you have to offer? Remember, any changes you make to self should be from the heart, and real. Interviewers can quickly read through the nonsense and by putting on an act or being fake to get a job only hurts you in the long run.

No one thinks of soft skills as an ability, but maybe we should. Let me ask this question: If you were to go to a new dentist's office, and he/she walks in with no teeth at all, would you let them work on your mouth? How about if you were going to get an exam and the doctor walks in with a full gold/diamond mouth grill and greets you with an obnoxious, "Heyyyyy" how far are you going to let him/her get with examining you? The honest answer to both questions, probably not very far.

How many times have you gone on an interview and thought you "aced" it, but you never heard back from the company? In your mind, the decision to hire you shouldn't be that hard. You need a job, there is one available, you should get it. Unfortunately, so many people have the same mindset. When in all honesty, your lack of preparation could be one reason why you were not offered the position.

It takes time to learn and develop soft-skills because they must become second nature. The following soft skills are transferrable both in the workplace and in your personal life. They are:

1. Empathy- the ability to recognize, understand and share feelings of someone else and not put them or the situation down.

2. Teamwork- the ability to work hand-in-hand with others to achieve a stated goal.

3. Communication- Both verbal and non-verbal communication are essential, and doing it effectively with others without ensuing arguments is a huge plus!

4. The ability to teach- sharing the information that you have learned over time regardless of if it's in the work setting or life can help someone else become better. In the workplace, remember, you can't be promoted if you can't be replaced.

5. Appropriate dress- fads change by the minute. A fad can range from clothing trends to body enhancers. As colorful and cool as it may seem, always ask yourself if it is appropriate for the workplace?

   When all else fails, business casual is always a good choice. Examples may be business slacks (or skirt) and a nice shirt, skirt and a nice pair of shoes.

Never go into an establishment as if you were going to a picnic or the club. It's just inappropriate.

6. Be positive! Another important detail to remember is to be positive. With a positive attitude, you can change minds, break barriers and alter behaviors of not only other people but yourself as well. If you are negative, the employer may think that you will bring a negative atmosphere filled with drama to the business place. By remaining positive, you increase your opportunity drastically.

7. Manners- It is important to have manners not just in a work setting, but in life. This is inclusive of being kind, how you conduct yourself and your behavior towards others. If you are difficult or don't present good manners during the interview, you probably won't use good manners at work. You never want anyone to single you out for being rude or difficult. Try to treat others the way you would want to be treated. Think before reacting.

Your soft skills show what you bring to the table from a human needs-based perspective. Soft skills can give a glimpse of what you will be like to work with, and how you may get along with team members, management, and clients.

Soft skills are just as important, if not more as hard skills. Soft skills are what can potentially get you in the door to show off your hard skills or what you can do. But without the ability to communicate, understand, look, smell and play the part, you probably won't get the part for which you are applying.

Your Image - *The Presentation of You*

When we first start dating someone, we go out of our way to look and act our best while attempting to present ourselves in a positive manner. The same thing should hold true when job hunting, and interviewing regardless if it's for a temporary or permanent position. It's your job to find a job and you never know who you may run into that can refer you to job leads. You should always go out of your way to look your best and be prepared to discuss employment opportunities with everyone you meet.

If you look polished and sharp, people you encounter will remember you for all of the right reasons and may be more likely to refer you if the opportunity arises. Keep these in mind:

- Personal hygiene is an overall statement of you. Most people like to smell good. But the key is to keep it simple. Don't overuse perfumes and colognes. Just because you like the smell, doesn't mean everyone will like it. Remember that perfumes can clash with other smells and can overload the room with negative impact. **Rule #1**: Be considerate and clean.

- Piercings and tattoos can be a statement, but it is a personal one. Is it appropriate for the job in which you are applying? Can they be covered if needed? Too much jewelry/tattoos can become an unnecessary distraction. **Rule #2:** When in doubt, do without or cover it up.

- Don't overdo the make-up or hair. It's another distracting feature that takes away from focusing on you. This is inclusive of bright overpowering colors (face and hair).

- Check yourself out head-to-toe in a mirror before you set out on your journey. Do you look like you're going to the club or a possible interview? **Rule #3**: Dress appropriately.

The Night Before the Interview

While it may not seem necessary, preparing the evening before an interview can be helpful to the start of your day and add to the success of your meeting.

The night before is a very good time to rehearse your responses to "general" questions one more time. Have you perfected elevator speech? You should be able to recite it very well, with no mistakes. Stand in front of a mirror, a friend or family member and say it! Make a recording and listen for places you can tweak and adjust. It should be a quick reflection of you!

Prepping also gives you the opportunity to figure out what you're going to wear, making sure everything is clean and pressed, eat a healthy dinner and get a good night's sleep. Take special time and care for yourself so that you can wake-up refreshed and ready for the day.

The Morning of the Interview

Regardless if you are putting in applications, or have a scheduled interview, <u>you should always dress as if an interview is going to happen</u>. You should also try to dress for the job in which you are applying.

Far too many times, candidates can fall short of expectations of the employer by not presenting themselves in a professional business manner. Help the interviewer see the type of employee you'll be by presenting the best you possible.

Whether it's a job working at a fast food restaurant or a position at a TV station, you have to care enough about how you look and present yourself so that you make a lasting good impression on the interviewer.

Clothing should be modest, clean and pressed. For men, appropriate clothing could be wearing a nice pair of dress slacks, a dress shirt (tie is optional) and dress shoes. For women, slacks or skirt (knee length), and blouse, an alternative would be a dress. As for shoes, if you are not used to wearing high heels, now is not the time to practice. A pair of flats that complement the outfit will be fine.

- Your hair should be combed, picked or brushed in a way that it is neat and presentable.
- Jewelry should be kept to a minimum. You don't want to be a show stopper with multiple pieces of huge dangling or flashy jewelry. It's unprofessional and unnecessary.

- Makeup if you wear it; should be natural looking. The goal is not to overwhelm the interviewer with your looks. Makeup is just an enhancer at this point.

16

- Look at yourself in a mirror before you leave. If you don't have a mirror, ask someone for an honest opinion.
- For the interview, skip the perfume or cologne. The interviewer may have allergies, and it could become distracting.

Self-Sabotage

You're ready for the interview. You've pumped yourself up, and this is a no-brainer because you are more than qualified for the job. Yesterday you felt prepared, but today, something just doesn't feel quite right? You brush it off thinking 'It's all in my mind.' You open the door of the interviewers' office and immediately freeze! Your mind isn't working the way you want it to, and your words aren't coming out the way you practiced. You do the best that you can, but you leave without an offer. You wonder what went wrong?

Many times, the *fear* of succeeding can take over leaving the subconscious mind to choose between deeply rooted emotions and logic. When this happens, emotions usually win leaving the mind to figure out how to get out of the situation. What comes next is called, self-sabotage. For every question the interviewer gives, your responses are short with no detail. You've lost the ability to focus and effectively communicate *how* you've gained the skills needed to perform this job. What's worse, you've lost the ability to sell you! So sitting in an office where you feel you don't belong, you try your hardest just to get it over with so you can go back to your comfort zone of the couch, Jerry Springer, and soggy cereal.

For any employer to want to hire you, first you need to believe in yourself and the skills that you have accumulated over your working or educational career. Then you need to learn how to sell those skills along with the product; which is you. Try to remember a time or a place where you have felt the most comfortable, successful and confident. Remember that place, and take that feeling everywhere you go! Think about that thought before the interview to put yourself in a positive frame of mind. Make this a habit!

Once you are feeling more confident, you can figure out who you are, and how your skills should be marketed to sell you for any job. Bottom line, why should someone take a chance on hiring you rather than someone else? If you find some of your hard skills are lacking, find a free class, go to the library or dust off your computer and work on making your skills a great selling point. If your soft skills need some work, try an etiquette class.

Ask yourself, "Am I marketable?" Do you have what an employer needs? If not, maybe it's time to brush up on those skills.

Regardless of the skills you need to improve, whether it's minor adjustments or a major overhaul, stay positive on your quest and find others who will encourage and help you.

The Interview

What is an interview? Most people sum it up as someone sitting behind a desk asking questions about past work experience. This is only partially correct. What makes a really good interview is someone who knows how to be a salesperson of themselves. Yes, in this very instant, you become the product, much like a commercial on television. You may be in competition with five other people for the same job. Why should you be hired over the others? What makes you unique and qualified? How would you answer that?

Your thirty-second elevator speech will come in handy. It should be robust enough to pull the interviewer in to want to know more about you. You should also be enthusiastic and authentic.

Communicating Effectively

Types of communication:
> Verbal
> Non-verbal (eye-contact, etc.)
> Interpersonal
> Written

Communication is the single most important skill of any interview or face-to-face meeting you will ever do in your life. The ability to talk to someone else about you.

A lot of people get nervous at the thought of public speaking (yes, this is a form of public speaking) because you are trying to inform and then persuade someone to hire you effectively.

Life is full of uncertainty that can include both positive and negatives. One thing for sure, however, is the ability to communicate both verbally and non-verbally can help give you more positive experiences than not.

When you communicate with confidence, it can help you get your point across, builds your credibility and helps others to trust what you're saying.

Take all modes of communication into consideration when dealing with others. By strengthening how you communicate, you can empower yourself to become more confident in your writing and speaking leading to different outcomes for your future.

Public Speaking Tips

Anytime you speak to another individual or a group of people; it is considered public speaking. Normally you don't get nervous when talking to your family and friends, but for some reason, most people get nervous when they have to speak in a formal setting. Here are some tips to help you get past the nervousness.

1. **Practice!** The biggest reason for nervousness is because you haven't planned what you're going to say and how you will say the material. Take the time to review and rehearse what you will say either in front of a mirror or someone else in a mock interview. This is one of the best strategies for speaking in front of others.

2. Don't use words that you don't fully understand. Although the word(s) may sound impressive, if you

can't articulate or use them correctly it will make you look ill-informed and not very smart.

3. Don't read from your resume or a cheat sheet. If you have been honest on your resume in the assessment of what you have done in the past, there is no need to read the material to the interviewer. You should know it.

4. Be credible by:
    a. Maintaining eye-contact
    b. Knowing what your mission/values are
    c. Being consistent and truthful with your answers

The RLS Method

This concept is an essential reminder of how you can put your best self forward when searching for a job. By utilizing the points listed, you may be able to increase your chances for gainful employment over those competing for the same position.

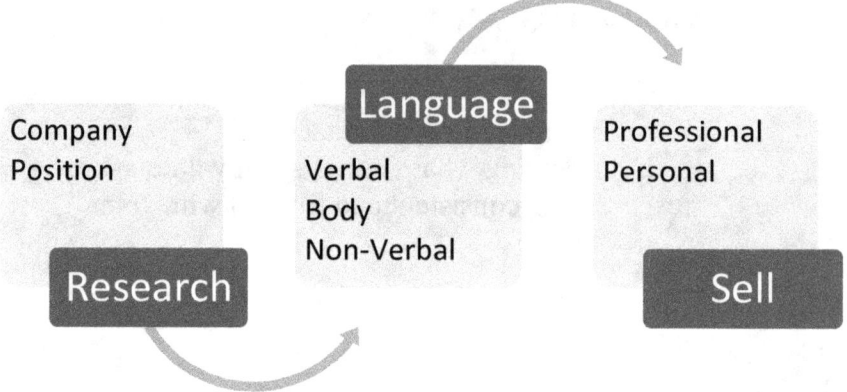

RESEARCH:

- Use Social Media to help you do your homework (Facebook, LinkedIn, Twitter).
- Does the company have a website? If they do, read it and know the company mission, practices and most of all what they do.
- Do you know what the position that you are applying for entails?
  - Can you quickly learn or brush-up on those duties if you are not familiar with them?
    - Read a book then practice the new skill.
  - Are you qualified through school or previous work experience?
    - Do you have certifications?
  - Can you get further education or training to qualify for this position?

LANGUAGE:

- How you present yourself is everything not just in the interview, but when you first walk in as well as when you're leaving. Don't forget how you come across on the phone is a big factor too!
- What type of language are you using – we all speak "differently" when in various situations. You never want to go into an interview and talk to the interviewer the same way you would with your personal friends.
  - Cussing, or using loud and obnoxious language is a no-no.
  - Sharing your personal business or problems is never a good idea.
- Do you know the language of your desired profession or business?
  - Are there technical names that should be familiar to you in this position?
  - Can you easily brush-up on recurring or new terminology that may be used in the position that you are applying?
- Your body language is just as important as what you say. It is the visual trademark impression that you leave with a possible employer.
  - Are you neat and clean? Clothes pressed, business casual and matching?
  - Did you take the time to prepare for the interview visually?
    - Your first impression (sight) could be your last if you're not careful.
  - If you are unsure of facial expressions, you may want to practice in front of a mirror. Weird faces and body movements can be a turn-off.
  - You should also be aware of your body, and the movements you make. How you sit in a chair. Do you cross your legs? What should

you do with your hands? Yes, these little details matter too!

SELL:

The overall goal is to show the interviewer who you are as well as what type of employee you will be for the company. Two main points are: selling yourself in a personal sense, as well as selling you – the business professional.

- Personally:
    - Who are you as an individual?
    - Are you positive in nature or are you negative?
    - Do you speak negatively about previous employers, or do you focus on what was "right" with the company and your co-workers?
    - Will you bring your home life (issues) to the workplace?
- Professionally:
    - What skills do you bring to the table that will enhance this company's bottom line?
    - What have you done (work-wise) in the industry that will contribute to what you will bring to this company?

Things to Remember

This part of the interview is all about building trust. When we meet someone, it's human nature to form a first impression on what you see, but then to form a second opinion on what you hear. You can alter what people think over a period-of-time; however, most job offers are made (and based) on the first impression of sight, and then of what they hear.

- Remember to be polite to everyone you meet in the office. Everyone in the office has something that you don't have; which is, a job. Being rude to one person can hurt your chances for that position. The first impression of you may be the last one you get to make. Be different!

- When asked "Tell me about yourself," about 75% of applicants respond with, "I'm hard-working, honest, reliable, and dependable. Use your rehearsed personal commercial.

- This is not the time to share your personal life (stories about your kids, what your mom does for a living or sob stories).

- This is your moment to shine – think about standing out from the norm.

- Look the interviewer in the eye! With this, you are forming an unspoken bond. You are building a sense of trust which is key. If you're talking to someone and they are looking all over the place rather than at you, how likely are you to believe what they are saying? Always be credible!

25

- Be as honest as you can with your answers, even when asked a difficult question, take a deep breath and speak at a relaxed pace. If you're not sure what is being asked, it is always better to ask for clarification of the question. An example, "I hear you asking...... is this right?" By asking this type of question, you are showing that you know how to ask for directions.

Many times, a candidate may have the qualifications and skills for a particular position, but they may not be offered the job. The reason can sometimes be as simple as how they presented themselves during the interview (speech or dress).

While it may seem unfair, it happens more times than one would think. First impressions count, make yours last.

Last Minute Tips Before the Interview

1. When you are going out to put in applications, dress as *if* you will be interviewed on the spot. Take every opportunity to make a positive impression by looking the part in which you are applying.

2. Turn your cell phone off or use silent mode.

3. If there is a receptionist, greet him/her and briefly explain the reason that you are there. If they are occupied (on the phone or with someone else), wait patiently until they are done.

4. Never take food or open drinks to an interview.

5.   You should always shake hands with the person who is interviewing you both before and after the interview. Thank them for their time and consideration.

6.   When you sit, do not put your personal belongings on the interviewer's desk. Either place your belongings on the floor beside you, or on your lap. If you keep your belongings on your lap, do not play or fiddle with them as that is distracting.

7.   Listen to the questions and take a moment to collect your thoughts before answering. Always be thoughtful in your responses rather than blurting out the first thing that comes to your mind.

8.   Be prepared to ask questions about the job you are interviewing for:
      a.   How soon are you looking to hire?
      b.   What additional skills are needed for the position?

9.   Be proactive. Before you leave, let the interviewer know that you look forward to hearing from them, and if they require further information, you are available for follow-up discussions either by phone or in person.

10.   Before leaving, again shake the interviewer's hand and thank them for the opportunity to interview.

11.   If there is a receptionist, make sure to thank him/her for their time.

12.   Follow-up with either a card, a brief letter, or email thanking them for time and again expressing your interest in the position.

Top 12 Reasons You May Be Overlooked

1. Are you prepared? (Dressed with resume in hand)

2. Did you exaggerate your skills? Be prepared to take tests to verify what you say you know.

3. Making or receiving calls or texting while at a job interview to schedule another job interview or converse with friends/family.

4. If you bad mouth your family, former managers, or previous jobs, what will you do to *this* company?

5. Being 10-15 minutes early is great. Even being on time is fine. But showing up an hour early insisting on being seen is not cool.

6. Don't be late. Leave early enough so that you have plenty of time to find the company and get yourself situated. There is rarely a good excuse for being late.

7. Never tell the interviewer that you gave up on something because someone you know took your idea and ran with it.

8. "I'm lazy, " or anything negative should never be an answer to any question during an interview. If

you're negative during the interview, the employer may feel that you would be negative on the job.

9. It's fine if you enjoy hanging with your friends, but telling the interviewer how you and your friends all picked up "charges" for bad girl/boy behavior isn't making them feel comfortable offering you the job. Personal moments like this should not be shared with a prospective employer.

10. Leave your friends, family and children at home. You are the one looking for employment.

11. Don't touch or grab things off of the desk of the person interviewing you. They are not your items, pictures, paperweights, etc. and you should never feel inclined to touch, move or play with them.

12. Lying on an application, resume, or during the interview is the biggest reason people don't get hired. Be honest in your skills, what you've done in the past, and what you can contribute if hired.

Remember, finding a job can be a job. It takes a lot of effort and perseverance. Believe in yourself, and be confident about what you have to offer.

www.ingramcontent.com/pod-product-compliance
Lightning Source LLC
Chambersburg PA
CBHW071835200526
45169CB00018B/1519